Also by Rev. Katie Rodriguez Banister

Aunt Katie's Visit (2003)

The Personal Care Attendant Guide (2007)

A Pocket of Poems and How to Write Your Own (2008)

Access-4-All, LLC.
PO Box 220751
St. Louis, Missouri 63122-0751
www.access-4-all.com; katie@access-4-all.com

First Edition, Printed in USA.

Karmic Validations: The Signs and Symbols along Your Way
By Rev. Katie Rodriguez Banister

Illustrations by Michelle Scott

Edited by:
Ligaya Figueras
Phyllis Banister
Steve Banister
Justine Dooley
Rev. Bill Duvendack

Cover and interior design by: Sue Sylvia, www.StaircasePressDesign.com

ISBN: 978-0-9744908-3-0
Library of Congress Control Number: 2010907188

KARMIC VALIDATIONS

The Signs and Symbols along Your Way

Rev. Katie Rodriguez Banister

Illustrated by
Michelle Scott

This book is dedicated to
those who seek answers
to thought-stirring questions.

The Universe
is communicating.

Are you
willing to listen?

LIFE WITH MY WIFE

Katie Rodriguez Banister is a woman of action. Her ideas get turned into books (this is her fourth), activities, PowerPoint presentations and speeches. Her energy and productivity are amazing. I've learned many things in my quest for true knowledge and the mysteries of the Universe. The main thing that makes the most sense to me is the idea that everything in existence is one with God. I think if we look close enough, we can see ourselves in everyone and everything we encounter. Katie is an expert on fairness. That's one of the many reasons I married her. She is concerned about how her actions affect others. That is why in this unique book Katie has included quotes from her friends and colleagues regarding their perspectives of the term "karma." Katie shows us how God is good and bad, light and dark, all beliefs, you and me: that ultimately, God is Love!

I've learned that birds are God's messengers. When I'm outside and see a feather on the ground, I pick it up, thank Father/Mother Sky for the gift of knowledge and open my intuition to receive messages. I've learned that everything that exists is an aspect of you and me. The bird is a part of me that is sending tools to me via God's infinite spirit. The knowledge I use to purposefully pick up the feather and thank Father/Mother God for the connection allows for more knowledge to enter me through divine means. Practicing our deep connection to Earth and all its inhabitants allows us to increase our capacity to expand our cache of knowledge. Using my intuition and having an awareness of Oneness is my way of listening to God. Karma is an outcome of positive or negative actions. If we act upon our intuition (from our heart) then we'll receive a positive or light/love karmic outcome. If we act upon our ego (from our fear center or fueled by hate) then we'll receive a negative or dark karmic outcome.

Just as humans are made up of billions of atoms, God/the Universe/the Divine Cosmos is made up of billions of souls. (Thank you to Rev. Ann Davies of BOTA for that idea.) Whether we are aware of it or not, each human has the same ultimate goal: to play the game of life in human form. If one isn't aware that life is a game, one is still playing it, regardless (although at a great disadvantage!). This game is very difficult at times, but it can be rewarding and fun as well.

The rules are thus:

1. Be aware you are playing the game of free will!
2. Ignore your ego and give up any fear, anger, hatreds, and negativity.
3. Understand that knowledge is power. Study world beliefs, quantum physics and spirituality. Find the loving side of all religions.
4. Understand that whatever your current situation, you are experiencing this life at this time because you are experiencing things as an agent of God/Divine Spirit.
5. Be happy you are alive; be happy your soul was allowed to come to Earth at this time, with all this technology available to us, enabling us to be very creative. Enjoy your life until you cross over and beyond.
6. Every moment is a lesson. No moment is ever the same. Find the value in every action!
7. Wake up, wake up, and wake up!

We are all pieces of God (souls) having experiences for the benefit of the whole of God, the infinite, multi-dimensional, vibrational Universe. Playing this game, as spirits manifested in human bodies, we all must make the choice to *wake up.*

Just because we are alive doesn't mean we are truly *awake*. You are not truly awake until you choose to learn more about the game and are willing to notice your progress on the game board called Earth. I give everyone permission to *wake up,* to invite Spirit in (in whatever guise you like) and love every experience; good *and* bad. Allow yourself to live in the now, for it is *never* not now.

The time has come for this book. More and more humans are waking up to the idea of Oneness. Karma and universal laws are making sense to more and more of us with each passing day. The days of the week are flying by. We no longer have time to read volumes of texts to understand the idea of karma. Katie Banister has provided a wonderful handbook; a quick reference guide for all of humanity to share.

Steven L. Banister

Astarian of the 8th Degree

ACKNOWLEDGMENTS

I have to thank my even-Steven, the man I have enjoyed for over seventeen years, married for ten of them. He has expanded my mind in directions I never would have on my own. He is my rock, my best friend, and a lot of fun.

This book would not have been born if not for the strong words of encouragement of our dear friends Rob and Marie Miller. Over dinner Rob asked, "Are you working on a new book?" I hemmed and hawed, "Well, I have an idea for a new one, but I'm tired of writing." Disregarding the last part of my comment he asked, "What's your subject?" I had to answer, "Karma." Rob said, "Katie, you have to write this book! It's going to be helpful to others."

Many people have contributed to this book. They include: Phyllis Banister, Dr. Alexia Hampton, Ellen Runge, Kay Kottemann, Mel Valdejo, Eileen Kiser, Jane Ahearn, Rev. Bill Duvendack, LySandra Strotheide, Alex Butterfield, Kimberly Anderson, Frank Gilner, Kim Swanson, Miki McKee-Koelsch, Melissa Humbarger, Scott Douglass, Robert Ferre, Nancy Reiter, Ernie Benecke, Leslie Elpers, Lisa Laird, Rhonda Macrum, Jerry Ballesteros, Pat Rodriguez, Nancy Nickolaus, Nick Ford, Jill Coon, Hal Maples, Cynthia Verdot, Judy Wanko, Deb Evans and Eddie Boster. I wish to thank Michelle Scott, my illustrator. She asked me what I had in mind. I gave her a few ideas but asked her to read the text and draw. Thank you Michelle for your sweet and simple artwork. You are all wonderful and caring people! Thank you for your contributions.

You may have noticed the title "Reverend" before my name. In the fall of 2008, Joy, a very fun and outgoing student I met through Washington University's Occupational Therapy program, told me she was going to get married. Then she asked if there was any certification I could get to perform her ceremony. That freaked me out a bit, but then I thought, "The Universe has brought me to this. I should do this." I looked online and found The Universal Life Church Monastery in Seattle, Washington where they honor all traditions and provide training, information, and resources for anyone to become a minister. Joy's mother was very upset about her daughter's decision and asked if a Catholic priest could perform traditional rituals with me. Well, I love collaboration and in the end, the ceremony was loving, creative, and just what Joy and her husband Jamie wanted. Since then, I've been asked to do another wedding and vow renewal ceremony. After my mother passed on, my family asked me to conduct her committal ceremony. It was a beautiful event and my mother's friend Maxine told me, "Katie, you have found your calling."

Editing credits to Ligaya Figueras, a woman who is serious about her craft; Phyllis Banister, my mother-in-law and loving woman; Justine Dooley, a very creative spirit; Steve Banister, a very soulful being; and Rev. Bill Duvendack, astrologer at www.418ascendant.com.

Thank you to Sue Sylvia of Staircase Press Design for her creative passion. She makes books and their covers look really good. Also thank you to the St. Louis Publishers Association for their knowledge, resources and programs that cater to the publishing community.

Finally, I would like to thank the Universe for giving me incredible situations from which to learn incredible lessons. I feel truly blessed. And by the way, I've changed personal names in examples throughout the book so that all beings may be happy.

TABLE OF CONTENTS

INTRODUCTION

I've read different definitions of karma and am a little confused by it. I'm interested in learning more about it.

– Disability advocate and community activist

Karmic validations affirm your choices from what to eat, what to wear, who you marry, what job to pursue and a million other decisions we make on a daily basis. My teens and twenties were full of shallow, empty and rotten relationships with guys. I cheated on them. They used me. But after my auto accident, which left me as a quadriplegic, I reinvented my perspective. Three years later, I found the man of my dreams. My wheelchair was the karmic validation I needed to get my act together in so many ways.

Why a book on karma? Well, I love the thought of knowing that I can contribute and affect the outcome of life here on Earth. What I think, say, and do on a daily basis creates the reality I live in. It took me many years to learn this, but better late than never.

In preparation for this book, I contacted sixty of my friends and business associates and thirty of them responded to the following questions:

Do you know of and believe in karma?

How do you define karma?

Do you have any examples of the effects of karma in your life?

Their responses are throughout this book and they ranged from "What the.......?" to "I'm with you on this."

Karma is somewhat easy to define. I typed the word "karma," clicked on my thesaurus, and the following words popped up: "providence," "coincidence," and "accident."

The theory of karma is a fundamental doctrine in Buddhism. This belief was prevalent in India before the advent of the Buddha. Nevertheless, it was the Buddha who explained and formulated this doctrine in the complete form in which we have it today. According to Buddhism, karma is the result of our own past actions and our own present doings. We ourselves are responsible for our own happiness and misery. We create our own heaven. We create our own hell. We are the architects of our own fate.

To the ordinary Buddhist, karma serves as a deterrent; to the intellectual, it serves as an incentive to do good. Therefore, a person becomes kind, tolerant, and considerate. The law of karma explains the problem of suffering, the mastery of so-called fate, the predestination of other religions and provides answers to all the inequality of mankind. Bad things are going to happen and I believe that the only control we have is our reaction to them. I think the goal should always be to find the beauty in what we perceive to be the bad.

Karma makes you responsible for your being. I can choose to love others and receive others or chose to hate and fear, receiving that in turn. Having knowledge lets us understand that everyone is a magician. A magician knows that knowledge is power, that we are all one, and being one we have *nothing* to hide or fear. We all need to *create* new experiences and play the game called *life*—not just the game on sale at the store, but real life!

YOU AND I MATTER

The definition of karma as a literal translation is "karma means action," and therefore every action is karmic. What creates positive or negative karma is our emotional tie to the action.

– Astrologer and cat lover

I want you to realize how important you are. You matter and don't you let ***anyone*** tell you differently. When we let others judge us we take on their judgments. We then give our power away. I say "we" because I'm human too. I'm not perfect nor do I claim to be. However, having lived forty-five years on this planet, twenty of those as a woman on wheels, including fifteen years of psychotherapy, and having married a sensitive and very spiritually based husband, I've gained awe-inspiring insights. All of our life experiences are opportunities to learn. We simply need to pay attention and learn the lessons.

I was born the day the St. Louis Cardinals won the World Series on October 15, 1964. This was my start to live a full and passionate life. I've always lived life with gusto. In fact, my 1983 high school class voted me, "Most likely to win an Oscar." (I may some day; never say never.) I put myself through college as a resident assistant for two and a half years and my parents helped out too. I earned my degree in recreation in 1987 and since then, I've always worked two or more jobs to make ends meet. I was hired as a recreation director for an apartment community on February 7, 1990 and four days later my life rolled into a completely different direction.

On a beautiful day in 1990, I was a passenger in an SUV that rolled over. The accident left me a quadriplegic and paralyzed from the chest down. I endured six months of hospitalization, fifteen months back at home with Mom and Dad, and I've been living on my own since 1992. Being the sixth of seven children has taught me how to thrive and survive. I learned how to do this with my determined free will.

Having free will separates humanity from animals. Having free will means you are a human with a soul. I feel that God created free will to allow us to play the game of life. This allows us to make personal decisions that affect our lives and those around us. What you do creates ripples that result in karma.

Karma governs the laws of the Universe around me. My actions have been determined to some degree or another based on a perception of the outcomes in the actual and spiritual world. This does not mean that I understand karmic laws based on Eastern religious models but more from a personal perception of what is good or not good.

– Spanish-speaking glass worker

WE ARE ONE

Karma is energy affecting this life or the next. I tend to try to "do good" by helping others but am not always successful. I like to think I am successful more than not (kind of my own personal karmic balance sheet.) I don't think of karma as a quid-pro-quo condition, but would like to think that someone will be there to help me when I need it.

When someone is evil, I like to think that "they will get their come-uppance" but I think my mind blends the concept of karma with the Christian concept of a reward for a well-lived life or punishment for the converse in the afterlife.

– IT specialist and married to her "perfect" partner

First and foremost is the realization that as members of planet Earth, we are connected beings in many ways. We are connected to the earth, ourselves, and all that is beyond our own being. We have a soul and so does the earth. We take care of the earth and it will take care of us; good or bad. To quote The Beatles from their song "I Am the Walrus" from the 1967 album *Magical Mystery Tour*:

"I am he
As you are he
As you are me
And we are all together."

My husband Steve is a big believer in a "we are all one" concept. He compares oneness to water. Every water molecule we drink, bathe in, water plants with, swim in, and dump pollution into is one with all water molecules. And we are one with all there is.

Humans are approximately seventy percent water
and water covers seventy percent of the earth!

All is water

All is everything

All is one

Unfortunately, we humans have a divide-and-conquer attitude that can separate us according to our religion, color, age, size, sexual orientation, and ability. I was at a recent celebration with friends, sitting next to the wife of a clergyman who was ignoring me. Her legs were crossed and her shoulder turned away. She was talking to everyone at the table but me. I guess she couldn't see past my disability or that I could be a happy and successful person. She was not going to be one with me—that was for sure! I have learned to accept the fact that there are people who cannot accept me. It's sad, but it's true.

I have seen countless examples that prove "we are one." For example, we all want and need many of the same things according to an American psychologist, Abraham Maslow (1908-1970.) Maslow's Hierarchy of Needs include:

Physiological needs — oxygen, food, water, and shelter.

Safety needs — secure and safe surroundings.

Needs of love, affection and belongingness — giving and receiving love and being part of a team.

Needs for esteem — self-esteem and respect from others.

Needs for self-actualization — the need to be and do that which a person was "born to do." "A musician must make music, an artist must paint, and a poet must write."

Now, in order to reach self-actualization, it takes consideration of those beyond the tip of our own nose. It means caring and sharing. But there is something that can trip us up big time. Read on…

Karma is what I am here to do.
My karma directs me towards overcoming ego,
being of service and sharing abundance
(not necessarily monetary.)

- Webmaster and professional choir member

THE EGO

From Hinduism and Buddhism: The total effect of a person's actions and conduct during the successive phases of the person's existence, regarded as determining the person's destiny. It appears that the hardships in life are tied to karma because they are lessons we need to learn, which is why they are happening to us in the first place. I'm not sure if there is a karmic lesson in a charmed life, because even an apparently charmed life has its difficulties. Everybody's going through something, right? It's just that some people's difficulties are apparent and those of others are not obvious, though they may be no less difficult.

– Spanish teacher and supermom of a challenged child

The Ego:

An inflated feeling of pride in your superiority to others

Consciousness of your own identity

Elements of our personality

Our ego can create great structures, art, music, books and on and on. My ego helps me face each day with a can-do attitude. I want to live. I want to be. But when I am focused only on me, I find myself alone at the end of the day and it is the ego that creates barriers and separates us from each other.

Beware that the ego tries to control our free will with fear, hatred, jealousy, selfishness to name a few of the ego's methods. Our higher self does not have to allow the ego to rule.

ME AND MY EGO

Why is it hard to just "Be?"
I trade the peace. I'm too busy.
The Universe tells me to settle down.
But I like going round and round.
I soon become ill
from doing too much.
Universal love
has lost its touch.
My paralysis left me sitting still.
But it can't stop
my own free will.

– Katie Rodriguez Banister

Finally, don't lose sight of the grand aspects the ego provides: confidence, fortitude, and resilience, and it allows us to step up to a challenge.

The ego, without a spiritual balance,
is the source of all of our harmful behaviors.

– Author unknown

SUFFERING IS A JUDGMENT

Karma manifests the fullest measure in the decisions we make. I define karma as Life/God allowing us to get what we think we want.

– Married to a woman on wheels and animal caretaker

The ego can fight, feel pain, and suffer. A fully enlightened soul may be aware of suffering, however never suffer or feel any pain on its own through knowledge and understanding.

This is a hard concept to keep in mind when I'm sitting in my dentist's chair. But on the flip side, I'm OK with sitting in my wheelchair, although some might see me as suffering. It's all relative to one's perspective. But please, keep the Novocain coming until I'm fully enlightened!

When I meet people for the first time, I often extend my hand, with paralyzed fingers, with the hope that they will extend their hand and we will form a momentary connection. But with some people, that is not possible to do. I see the sad and pitiful look in their eyes as I come near them. I catch them staring and when I look back, they turn away. They see me as less than they are. Now, in some ways, yes, I can move less of my body than they can but it doesn't make me less of a human being.

I've now learned that one of my roles in this lifetime is to teach others about compassion. I need help to do just about everything: to eat, to dress, to care for my body's most intimate needs as well as transportation, to care for my house, and to manage my finances. I have no real privacy, and I need caring people around me every five hours because that's how long my bladder will hold out before I need someone to insert a tube in my urethra to give me relief. Some folks keep a tube in all the time, attached to a leg bag of some sort. But I'd rather get out of my chair every five hours and do intermittent catheterization (or as I call it, "my cath").

OK, I may have shared too much information with you, but that's exactly my point here. Try not to feel shame or sorrow for me. I'm not suffering. I'm just living the best life I can and need other's help to do so. I want help, not pity.

I know I'm working off karma here. Karma is in full swing. As I mentioned earlier, I was pretty selfish in my earlier years. I did more for me than anyone and I wasn't very thankful. But I know now that if I can face every day with an attitude of gratitude and I am in service to others, life brings me what I need.

Every night, after my aide has gotten me tucked in bed during the week, or Steve has on the weekends, I say, "Mother Goddess and Father God, thank you for ____." I share three or four things that happened that day for which I was grateful. It sets the tone for a great night's sleep—unless I get too excited and then it takes me some time to calm down and relax, which happens frequently. I wouldn't sleep given the choice because there is always so much to do. But If I don't sleep, the next day can be unbearable.

Karma is what you put out in the world that comes back to you. I have always believed in karma and tried to be helpful to people every day. Last year, I was diagnosed with stage two breast cancer and had a bilateral mastectomy, and chemo and radiation treatment. I was humbled by all of the prayers, gifts, support, food, and money that friends, family, and strangers gave to me. You never know what will happen so be prepared to keep the kindness flowing!

– Talent agent and mother

GOD

I believe in karma and know that when I start my morning in a pissy mood, complaining, refusing to give thanks for my job, my home, my friends, and all that I have, I find that the Universe has a way of giving me every red light, traffic jams, spilled coffee, and trouble galore.

And I've also learned that on my walks along the beach, picking up cigarette butts may lead me to the perfect shell.

– Social justice worker and avid chocolate lover

Just about every culture has a belief in a God. There are differences, though, in their look and stories of each belief, religion, etc. Thus, (the Virgin) Mary (Christian) is Durga (Hindu) is Isis (Egyptian). Similarly, Jesus (Christian) is Krishna (Hindu) is Osiris (Egyptian) is Buddha (Buddhism). It all works like the spokes of a wheel of many paths leading to the same point.

If you believe that God created everything, then everything is God—the good, the bad, and everything in between. You are God. I am God. It matters not your religion. In fact, there are some big egos in many of our religious traditions today. It's like, "If you don't agree with me, you are WRONG!" With this thought process, there is little room for discussion or tolerance at all. It saddens me that people exclude others because of a difference of opinion. One of my mother's favorite sayings was, "That's why there's chocolate ***and*** vanilla."

My truth tells me that in the beginning, God set up a basic plan and then left it up to us to figure out the details for ourselves. I ask you, have you ever had a teacher hand out a test with all the answers on it, marked with an A+

and your name was already on it? No, I didn't think so!

God is learning from our experiences, as we are too. Events are in motion to teach us the lessons we need to learn for our personal growth. I like to think that we are "God's market research." My mother and I worked for a company doing opinion polls for food products, shampoos, commercials, and any other product a company wanted to be evaluated by the public. Yes, we were those people in the mall with a clipboard in hand asking, "Can I ask you a few questions today?" We were often ignored but always found kind souls who would share twenty minutes or more of their time with us. I loved the food-tasting studies; they were the most fun!

Market research reinforces the value of opinion and we are all entitled to our own perceptions. For instance, if you don't like lima beans, are you going to let someone force you to eat them? (This doesn't count the times our mothers made us try new foods as children.) If you don't like wearing the color chartreuse, will you allow someone to force you to wear it? (This doesn't count if you join a group and that's the color of their uniforms.) The answers to these questions would most likely be no (unless you are a people pleaser and that's a whole other book.) But that's the same way I feel about God. What's right for me may not be right for you. Everyone should be allowed to honor God as they see fit.

The real question is: Will you slow down enough to listen to this great entity within and around you?

Less than a year after my accident, a family friend called and asked me to come speak to her high school class about my life on wheels. My sister Eileen loaded me and my manual wheelchair into her car in a rainstorm and drove me there. I talked a while and left plenty of time for questions and answers. I had fun and had found my calling. God was in the house!

In many of my presentations over the past eighteen years, people have asked me, "Regarding your disability Katie, are you mad at God?" My response is always no. I don't think God caused the accident that left me paralyzed from the chest and down. I don't think God's that mean. I also don't think the accident was caused for a reason. I think the accident happened as a result of living in the third dimension. It just happened and it was up to me to make *reason of it.* I want to be a ***victor*** of my circumstances and not a victim. Life is a free will zone. We all make choices and then we must live with the repercussions.

Being a victim brings on nothing but despair, sadness, depression, and negative situations. I want positive energy surrounding me. I'm not perfect, but if I put forth positive energy, I receive such in return.

The vibrations you create have a reciprocal effect
so that you have a direct experience
of what you are creating.

– Graphic artist and energy worker

REINCARNATION

I've been here before. I just know it!

– Dancer and recreation professional

For me, reincarnation makes sense. I also agree that you can believe in just one life per person and still believe in the principals of karma. But deep inside of me, I know I've been here before. I just know it. For example, there are people who can pick up an instrument and play it. They can play without a lesson or any training; they can just do it. This could be seen as a talent one mastered in a past life. Another example is a friend of mine who hated going to high school. She would miss class (some for legitimate reasons, sometimes not) and rarely ever studied, yet she aced every test she took. It made her teachers suspect that she was cheating but they had no proof. Some people have got it. Some people don't. My friend knew what she knew. She just knew it!

I believe that God created dharma, our path, a movable structure. Our soul's free will is our incarnation, fluid with the decisions we make or don't make. I know what I am now is what I used to be. But we grow from experience in each new lifetime. I believe that the reason we are not able to fully remember our past lives is because we need to be concerned with our present life. Now. Right now!

When it comes to karma the spiritualist believes in evolution and compensation. The scientist believes in cause and effect. Both are right.

In the book *Karma: The Mechanism Create Your Own Fate,* Herman Kuhn states, "Reincarnation manifests our craving the physical experience, all the values, ideas, and ideals we carry deep within us." He, too, feels that life is an

adventure and you should have fun seeking answers. That is probably why I chose a degree in recreation—I love fun!

Carpe diem is Latin for "Seize the day." (When I was in middle school, I owned a t-shirt printed with that motto and I loved wearing it.) Seizing the day is what you must do in order to make this lifetime the best that it can be, and to help advance your soul in the next lifetime.

You do this by:

Being aware of your surroundings, tuning in to what is really going on in your life.

Make choices, and not just the easy ones. It is through the most difficult experiences that we learn the most.

Create a list of things you ***really*** want to accomplish. Don't evaluate the list, just make the list. Then, ***act*** on one of the adventures on your list by figuring out how to lovingly, honestly, and creatively make it happen.

Ask for help, and ask in a way that someone will want to give it to you. Demanding assistance is no way to get it.

The Universe listens and responds in turn.

Let go of fear. Turn off the TV (that's a hard one for me too) and if you have to watch the news, do so with the knowledge that the telecast is a reflection of those who produce it. You don't have to think as they do.

KARMIC LAWS AND INFLUENCES

Karma: When "things" happen in conjunction; when there is no apparent relationship one to the other, also happenstance. Most recently, when we had lived at a house numbered 605, we moved into an apartment numbered 560. To me, this use of numbers bodes well for the future, and is an example of karma – and instance of similarities.

– Methodist and grandmother of four

By now, you have read many different interpretations of karma. Whether you believe in one lifetime per person or continuous life times, our earthly mission is to do good and work from love. But there are basic laws at work here. They are defined in different ways by different people. I'm giving you my perspective, but by all means search further for the answers that meet your needs.

I believe that our soul enters body after body, learning lesson after lesson. I accept as truth the Universal Laws. (See Appendix A.) These are laws of nature, personal action, and cause and effect. For example, the Law of Return is about experiencing birth after birth and that life is cyclical. Hence, what goes around comes around. Further, karma causes the return. It is the Law of Adjustment that keeps things in balance. The Law of Giving supersedes taking and you can't simply give to get. Finally, you know how Lady Justice stands holding her scales in balance and wears a blindfold? Well, think of karma as having the blindfold removed. What is, is. The Universe never claimed to be fair and when you put demands on the Universe, I don't think you'll be pleased with the outcome. Every one of your thoughts and actions causes a reaction. Consider the outcome as cosmic payment.

Ministers Earlyne and Robert Chaney feel that obstacles are great opportunities for karmic growth. Karma is a teacher, liberator, giving conscious reminders that develop our character. I feel the same way. My paralysis gave me a mission on Earth. I found my passion as an author, which is totally freaky because I dreaded my English classes and my grades were barely at a C level. But I have learned to ask others to critique my work to make me a better writer. I'm not a fancy writer and in fact, many people have shared their appreciation of how easy it is to read my books. Thanks, Universe!

KARMIC VALIDATIONS

Karma is fate and/or the Universe playing a part in our lives by forcing people to deal with, and hopefully acknowledge, how their actions affect others. My grandmother told me that adults who were difficult children get children of their own who are just as difficult or worse so that they can experience what their parents went through.

– Twelve-year-old girl with a seasoned soul

God is speaking, are you listening? Are you paying attention to what is going on in your head, your body, and the world around you? Are you finding the clues along your path to help you make healthy decisions? Are you finding answers?

Karmic validations are signs and symbols along your life's path. A karmic validation reinforces the decisions you make. If you make a decision from your heart, act upon it. If it makes you feel good, more than likely, you are where you need to be. If you make hurtful, negative, and damaging decisions, karma will give you what you asked for and chances are you'll feel sad, let down, angry, and depressed. Our ego loves for us to be focused on fear of life and our surroundings. Instead, fear nothing!

A karmic validation I most recently experienced was with the publication date of my third book, *A Pocket of Poems and How to Write Your Own*. The U.S. Copyright Office gave my poetry book the publication date of

February 11, 2008. That is exactly the date my injury happened in 1990. That is the Universe clearly validating and creatively reminding me that I am right on track with my life's mission. I think karmic validations are life's communications. They encourage or give warnings and it is up to us as individuals to uniquely interpret their meanings. There are no coincidences.

Finally, I think déjà vu is the ultimate karmic validation because when it happens, it feels so real. Déjà vu is the feeling of having been somewhere, met someone, or said something that you knew in your logical mind had not occurred, but in your current life, you can't help thinking and feeling it had taken place. Your brain says, "No way!" and your soul answers, "Way!"

I believe in karma, both individual soul karma and Universal/ humankind karma, or collective conscious karma. For example, the events of 9/11: I do not necessarily believe that every human being either in the air, in the towers, or on the ground was meant to die, but I do believe that it happened because of a collective group conscious decision which resulted in a huge amount of negative karma being released into our Universe. That karma affected more than those planning that attack could have foreseen.

– Recreation provider and mental healthcare worker

ME AND MY KARMA

I feel that karma/karmic issues are life lessons that we agree to take on in a lifetime (incarnation) – and that we are subject to that lifetime (incarnation). We earn or agree to it, and it's always a lesson of some sort or another. Everything is karma.

– Shopkeeper of ceremonial traditions, resources, and information

Below are true instances that validate the power of karma in my life. It's all kind of freaky, but cool nonetheless.

I hired Marcie as a night attendant and things started out great, but after about three weeks, things changed. Marcie would arrive late and I called her attention to it. She improved, but had a snippy attitude every night after that. It got to a point where she could do the physical duties of her job in a very cold and impersonal way, but I really couldn't fire her for that. Marcie had taken off a few nights over the December holidays. Steve filled in and didn't mind doing so. The night Marcie was to come back, I took a deep breath and said to Steve, "Oh well, I guess I have to see Marcie tonight," when inside I was wishing I didn't have to.

Marcie undressed me and was helping me empty my bladder when she coldly announced, "Well, I don't know how to say this other than to let you know I'm giving you my two-week notice." I was mad, not because she was leaving, but because she did so in my most vulnerable state. Why couldn't she have told me when I was clothed and in my chair? In the end, I was ecstatic to see her go ***and*** I found an aide the following week. In fact, I found Karen, an even better aide; she was spiritual, loving, and get this: after her second week with me, she left a card on my desk thanking me for hiring her. So I had to endure Marcie to get to Karen.

On my way to my friend Melissa's party, with Steve at the wheel, I asked out loud, "Universe, please send me a person who designs public relation materials." Our company, Access-4-All, was going through a few changes and we needed updated materials. Steve's reply was, "Well you go, girl!" We arrived at Melissa and Derric's apartment. There were lots of folks there but I saw an open spot for my wheelchair and rolled over to meet Sherry. And yes, you guessed it; she designs PR materials and works for a local nonprofit group. She checked out my Web site, www.access-4-all.com, and is looking forward to helping my cause. Pretty trippy, huh?

Steve and I went van shopping at a local dealership and were shown a Dodge Sprinter. It was fully loaded with all that we wanted and priced lower than the base price of a current year model. I asked, "Can you put a tow package on it?" I got a yes and then asked, "Will the price you gave me be the final price?" I got another yes and was told, "Oh, you'll be eligible for the mobility discount through our national office and get $500 back because you're in a wheelchair." I then told him I'd take it. Because it was a 2006 model, the dealership was going to go over the vehicle in detail, put a new battery in it, and give it a good wash.

About two weeks later, I went to pay for and pick up my new van. The salesman said, "Oh, my boss says the tow package is an extra $500." I was fuming inside but weak at the same time and bought it anyway. Buying vehicles can be an intimidating venture. I wish I had had the nerve to question the man, but I didn't. The next week I called the national office to process my rebate. They told me it was good on new vehicles only. My van was sold to me as new and had only 70 miles on it but they disagreed. I then called my original salesman's boss to follow through on this. I was told that they would talk to the national office. I waited two months, calling every week to check in. Finally, I received a check of $500 from the local dealership. I find it funny that the place that "stole" $500 from me had to pay it back themselves. Oh, about a year later I ran into that same salesman at a restaurant.

He told me he lost his sales job and was working as an administrator at a local school and seemed somewhat unhappy. Ain't karma a b-t-h?

KATIE BELIEVES

ALL THINGS ARE POSSIBLE IF YOU

REMEMBER TO

MAKE HEALTHY AND HELPFUL DECISIONS

AND LOVE THE PROCESS

What goes around does not always come around
but it's still good advice to act like it will.

– Property manager and percussionist

KNEE-DEEP IN JUDGMENT

Karma and reincarnation go together.
It means that things that happen in a current life
can be caused by actions in previous lives.
I feel this is just the nature of things and that
there isn't a great karma judge up in the sky somewhere who
says, "You were a bad boy. Next lifetime, you get to be a frog."
I don't believe in sin or judgment.
I don't think cause and effect or karma is even classified
as good or bad.
Karma isn't punishment.
It is just the inevitable effect from our action.
We are emitting carbon dioxide but don't seem to realize
that the coastlines will be devastated by
rising water when the ice caps melt.
Whose fault is it?
Looking at the abuses and greed and fraud
in our economic system,
one could have predicted that eventually
the house of cards would have to fall.
Our actions will be accounted for.
With karma, even if we don't get caught
being bad now, it may still be regretted later.

– Labyrinth builder and lover of life

It appears that our need to judge our life and others can get in the way of living a peaceful state of being. My father was very critical. If there was a hair out of place, he would tell you so and it had better be corrected to meet his expectations.

Our given families by birth can be a pain in the rear. They can be a wonderful support system and break you down as well. We are often critical of our own family members. I know I can be. My father raised his children to be Indian chiefs, not followers. The consequence is quarreling, bickering, control and micromanaging. On the other hand, when a crisis hits us, my siblings and I are up and ready to tackle it head on.

But age and disability have taught me that life isn't about perfection. Life is messy. You're going to get dirty. I do like things to be as neat and orderly as possible but I've discovered that it's not possible in all situations. I've learned to cut myself some slack and to do so for others as well, especially when it comes to family. The true beauty of your birth family is that they are an incredible testing ground for patience, understanding, and group participation. And if you can love your family, you can love anyone!

There is another family that we are members of, and that's our soul family. Have you ever met someone with whom you felt an instant connection?

Have you looked into their eyes and felt a true connection at that first meeting? This doesn't mean being out and about, kissing anyone looking at you. I've been down that path and found dead-end relationships.

A soul family member doesn't judge you, they just like being in your presence, sharing time and space. One thing that is frustrating for me is that my soul family is as busy and energetic as I am, and we have a hard time getting together because of our schedules. So I've learned to cherish these loving and important people and enjoy whatever comes my way.

SERVING AS A WITNESS

When I was a little girl, my father introduced me to and defined the concept of karma as "energy of attraction." If a person is dark, they attract dark, if a person is light, they attract light, etc. We are all part of a whole. I need to be surrounded by good energy because I am very sensitive!!

– Dance instructor and business owner

I'm a fixer. I like to fix what I perceive to be wrong. In the past, when I saw someone struggling, sad, or depressed, my response was to assume the cheerleader role saying things like, "Come on. Snap out of it. You're OK. Don't stress." But now, I've learned to simply be a witness; to observe. Just observe. Now, when someone asks me for an open ear, I'll gladly give it. But times of struggle are where we have opportunities to learn some of our best lessons. I wish I could fix everyone's problems but I can't and I shouldn't.

PERCEPTION

When it comes to believing in karma, I fall into the "sort of" category because you can put bad stuff out into the Universe and have good stuff come back to you, and vice versa. I do not think the Universe is consistent in this regard.

– Executive administrator and mother of three

The most important aspect of karmic validations is how *you* interpret them.

You are the judge and jury of your actions. You can ask others for their thoughts; I know I do—sometimes so much so that I've let their opinions influence my decisions. But the messages the Universe is sending you require your full attention and for you to come to your own conclusions.

We have doctors, lawyers, teachers, police officers, therapists, and a whole host of other advisors and community members to guide us and our life. Utilize and adhere to these resources but take the time necessary to figure out things for yourself.

Karmic validations affirm your decisions with a positive or negative result. I aim to live in a positive, light-filled life and avoid the negative, dark side of being, although greatness can come from difficulty. I'm sharing my light and dark with the hope it is helping you in some way.

HAPPINESS IS AN OPTION

Karma is energy each of us has that cannot be seen but which interacts with other people's energy. Someone with negative energy will never have peace. I have experienced situations where I did an unselfish thing and was rewarded later by someone unselfishly doing something for my benefit.

– Legal professional and actor

During the end of my six months of rehabilitation, I remember that these two guys in rehab with me would always ask me, "Katie, why are you always so damn happy?" I just smiled, shrugged my shoulders, and did what my physical and occupational therapists told me to do. Mom used to say, "You catch more flies with honey than vinegar!"

Because I choose more often to be positive in my given situation, people often forget how disabled I really am. They complain to me about how hard their life is and how unfair it can be. How they "can't do what they used to." This can become a difficult conversation for me. My paralyzed life is a daily struggle. I recently had a bout with insomnia. Imagine lying awake at three in the morning…sleepless and you can't get out of bed because you can't move your body on your own; can't get up and watch TV or pick up a book to read or work on your computer. I don't play the paralysis card often, but it is my reality. Therefore it is hard for me to go down that path with people since I

need someone to move me, empty my bladder, wipe my buns, dress me, and prepare all my meals for me. But I'm really not bitter. This is karma in my life that I'm learning how to live with every day.

People have the perception that because I received a settlement, my life is a piece of cake. But it took ten years of living on Medicaid and food stamps and enduring two trials, one in 1995 and the other 1997. I know of living with less. And worse, the opposing council obtained my therapist's notes and tried to paint me as "a girl that got what she deserved." Now really, we all have skeletons in our closets; things we don't want others to know, things we're not proud of doing. But I stood my legal ground and thank God the judge ruled out using such intimate information. What happened back in the 1980s had little to do with my accident in 1990. And, my therapist, Susan, learned never again to take such detailed notes on her clients.

Through it all, I chose to mostly maintain a positive attitude. While I waited for my case to come to an end, my family contributed money so that I could live independently. What was really great was repaying my siblings every dollar once I could. I'm not happy 24/7 but I have learned to always try to make the best of every situation.

ECONOMIC KARMA

If we define karma as a force in the Universe that moves us toward our destinies, then the Yiddish word beshiert would be similar. An example is how I met my wife. Because the class I wanted to take at Brooklyn College was closed, I signed up for a class I didn't need but that sounded interesting. It turned out to be a class my future wife needed for her major. We met, dated, and married.

—Psychologist and father of four

The recent economic shake-up and subsequent job losses could be seen as an aspect of the earth's soul, as our planetary soul (vs. our personal soul) "creating" a shift.

When people are forced to change and create a new life or paradigm (loss of job = big life change) it gives many souls the opportunity to wake up to the light and gain awareness that they can create something new. And they wouldn't have been able to make such a shift had they kept the same job or routine.

If you have lost your job, this may be hard to comprehend, but you have been given the gift of time. OK, how is time going to help you? It will. Let me use this example from my own life: If my accident hadn't slowed me down, my life would not be what it is today. I was "ripp'n and runn'n" back in the day and I used to be pretty selfish and shallow when it came to relationships and my work habits. I was trying but floundering. Then my car accident happened in 1990 and sent my life in a new direction. As I stated previously, it took six months of hospitalization and living with my parents for fifteen months before I began living independently in 1992. I lived on

food stamps and public aid while working part time. I learned to take time to recover from my losses because change takes time.

So how do you put dinner on the table? Let's say that you see someone struggling to carry bags or boxes and you ask him if he needs help. He says yes, you help him, you begin to chat and you end up making an acquaintance. You inform this person (in a sincere rather than whiney way) that you have lost your job, times are tough and you are looking but haven't found the right opportunity. You may find that this person may have a lead for a job or know of places that could help you. If you come from a place of "I want to help myself" you are more likely to find it. To quote a guest on *The Oprah Winfrey Show*, "I feel better when I've gotten hand-ups instead of handouts." I'm willing to do what needs to be done and you can do this too. You can. Really, you can.

I have a friend, Ann, whose partner, Daisy, lost her job with a very well-known company, where she was employed for twenty-plus years and pretty high on the salary scale. Daisy was immediately devastated and Ann did her best to comfort her. A few months later, we were all at a party. Daisy entered the room and wow did she look good. She told me that she had started gardening more to save on groceries and that the added bonus was her healthy tan. I told her, "The energy around you is awesome." She answered, "You are not the only one who has said that to me." Remember, when something challenging happens to you, strive to find the beauty in the bad.

A higher power is often referred to as "The Creator." If the creator created everything, then you are a creator too. Think out of the box, out of the ordinary—and create the next ______________. (You fill in the blank.)

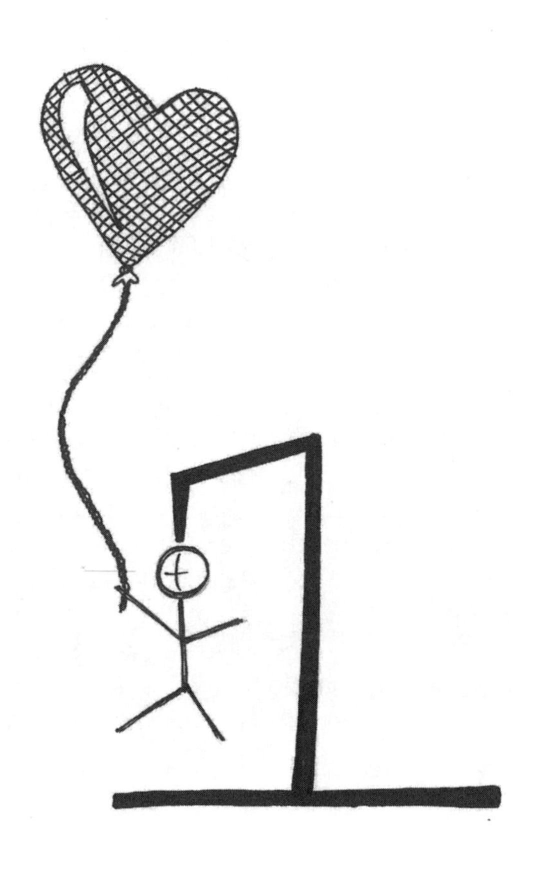

ADDICTION, THE GREAT SABOTEUR: THE EGO AS KING AND QUEEN

I believe karma is the thought that the behaviors you engage in now affect your future self.

– Mental healthcare employee and caring woman

My very dear friend Ben called with tears in his voice and said, "Katie, I need Steve to take me to the hospital." The following questions couldn't come out of my mouth fast enough:

"Are you OK? Are you hurt? Should I call an ambulance?"

"No," Ben assured me. "I…well…"

I responded, "What? What can I do?"

"Well, it's substance abuse. I—," he stammered.

I reassured him, "It's OK, what do you need?"

"I need to go someplace—someplace that can help me. And could you watch my dog?"

How could I not help? Here was a human being admitting his fault and asking me for help. Steve drove over to Ben's, picked him and his dog Asia up, took Ben to a rehabilitation facility, and returned home with our temporary roommate on four legs. Ben's recovery isn't going to be easy but he took a huge step with that telephone call.

Addictions are the ego at its worst. Addiction is running away from problems and life and not forgiving yourself or others. It takes a person out of balance. We (I'm no angel here, I'm a workaholic) can become addicted to food, money, sex, work, power, emotions, drugs or alcohol, pain or abuse, possessions, consumption, shopping, cleaning, or organizing. Yes, a person can be addicted to just about anything. *Webster's New Collegiate Dictionary* defines addiction as, "A compulsive physiological need for a habit-forming substance." Whatever!?

I met my therapist, Susan, in 1990 through a family friend. I was twenty-five and was happy on the outside but miserable on the inside. I didn't want to take the time to figure out why I wasn't happy, but I knew I wasn't. I kept myself busy with rotten relationships with men. They used me, I used them, and all of them fizzled out with time. In addition, I couldn't find a job that would give me what I wanted. I was restless and didn't know why. My first week of therapy, I handed Susan a list of thirty things I needed to change about myself. Her response was, "We'd better get busy!"

I think my addictions were to sex and to my emotions. I say "were" because it was through Susan's help that I am more at peace with these two issues. I lost my virginity at sixteen to a guy I really loved. The only problem was, I began to enjoy sex with him, him, him, oh… and him, too! My therapy and disability slowed me down enough though to find a more loving relationship. And while I am still a very emotional person (I can cry during a TV commercial) I've learned not to go off the deep end by not getting as mad as I used to.

Ben got out of rehab and I helped in ways that I could. But I will not be taken advantage of. The worst thing you can do for addicts is cater to their every need. If people are serious about overcoming their addictions, they will want to help themselves. I will not be an enabler by making excuses for irresponsible actions, allowing people to shirk their responsibilities, or do more for them than they can themselves. However, this doesn't mean I'm heartless. Substance abuse has affected Ben's memory, especially his short-term memory, so I have to be a little more understanding when he forgets things. He has physical pain and uses beta-blocker medications and should not take pain killers. His path is not easy but he must find a way to constructively and positively deal with what is before him.

One of the best ways a person can overcome an addition, according to Dr. Drew Pinsky, the counselor to the famous on the shows *Celebrity Rehab* and *Sober House*, is to start thinking and feeling good because when you start thinking and feeling bad, you are going to use again. It's not about being a good or bad person, it's about how you navigate life soberly.

Sobriety can also be successful when the blaming stops. The past is past. What Mom or Dad did or didn't do is over. Let go and live in the now!

My friend Bill was editing this book and informed me that I had left my own addiction off the list. (I subsequently added it.) I am addicted to work — thanks Dad for the inheritance! My work addiction is a constant issue. I will write, give presentations, consult, and volunteer until it sometimes makes me sick with bladder infections, stomach aches, and heartburn. Before I know it, the day is gone, most of the evening is gone and I'm still in my office typing away on my keyboard. Fortunately, I married a man who yells from the living room, "Katie, it's late. Get out of your office!" Am I lucky or what?

Finally, dismiss the ego from a commanding position. Instead, rule with your heart. Your free will is precious. Use it wisely!

EXPECTATION VS. HOPE

You can't do the right thing just because you expect a reward, either here or in the hereafter. You do it simply because it's the right thing to do. And if that's your true motivation, then karma will reward you fully.

– Mother and crafty creator

For me, karma is the reflection of my thoughts or actions reflected back upon me in some way at some time. In my younger years, I thought it would be really cool to have grey at the temples like Reed Richards in Fantastic Four and now I do!

– Graphic artist and music lover in Texas

When you tell the Universe, "I am good. I do good. I expect good in return," you are setting yourself up for a lot of disappointments. You can't expect anything. Dr. Wayne Dyer, one of my favorite authors and speakers, stated in his movie *Ambition to Meaning* that there are two musts for any self-actualized person: Detachment of outcome and independence of the good opinion of other people.

First, you can't do just to get. It's that simple. Give of yourself because of love, respect, and honoring another, and not what you may get out of the deal or transaction. Give freely of yourself without expectation. Since we are all one, your gift to another is a gift to yourself.

Second, don't allow the judgment of others to influence your being. This one is hard for me. If I put on a new outfit or change my hair color, my husband had better notice! But he often doesn't. So instead, I should be happy with my own approval. I look in the mirror and find a way to love me, as is. I'm comforted by the thought, though, that even supermodels get a pimple. But if they have one, I'm sure it's air brushed out when the ad goes to print. Wouldn't it be cool to have your own permanent air brush? I'd use it every day!

Being of service to others makes karmic sense. For example, at some restaurants, the wait staff thinks lowly of their profession. I say, "No way!" You are bringing food to those who need it! A mechanic may think she's less, but young lady, you are fixing something that another cannot! Service is not just work-related. Being kind to other human beings and animals and helping because you *want* to with a good attitude is the important thing. Service to others is where it's at. Lovingly and willingly help another and you will receive it in some form, too. It may not be exactly what you want, but it will have its worth.

Finally, what we think we want is not always what we need at that moment on a soul level. The ego often misleads us through our expectations. Karma provides us with what we need on a soul level versus what our ego thinks we need, enabling us to grow to our full potential. That darn ego!

Having this understanding of what karma truly is helps us to accept the world in which we live. This is true responsibility. Karma is Sanskrit for "action" and it isn't something you can always walk away from. No one can escape karma until you leave the third dimension. Karma will keep bringing similar experiences your way until you choose to deal with the situation at hand and learn from it.

Start thinking beyond yourself and expect nothing in return.

GIVING IS RECEIVING

I know of and believe in karma, although not to the extent that I include it as part of my religious faith. I would define karma as loosely the old saying "what goes around, comes around."

– Accountant and car enthusiast

I had to share this story from one of my friends in an email he sent, responding to one of my questions:

"I have a very recent example of karma in my life to share with you. It is odd that you ask today because yesterday I got a very big reward for something I did thirty-some years ago. In 1978, I bought a Guild acoustic guitar from a very good friend when he was really broke and I was only slightly better off (as I've always been). A few years later a band mate (who later left his wife and kids to break up my love relationship) left that guitar in an unsafe place that left it damaged. I had it fixed and it busted again. I fixed it again but it broke again, so I just gave up. I had a beautiful yet useless guitar.

Over the holiday season in 2008, I got to talk to my old friend from whom I had originally bought the guitar and told him all that had transpired. Yesterday, I received in the mail a Guild guitar EXACTLY like the one I fought so hard to save with a note saying what a good friend I had been to him and how much it meant to him that I bought that guitar from him when he was down even though I really could not afford to help him.

He has done well for himself financially since those years when we were young, broke, aspiring musicians. He wanted to do this for me. This is how I see karma, as a word used to describe the occasional event when something you do comes back to you in a way that repays your actions."

YOUR KARMA ACCOUNT

Karma is a spiritual presence that keeps things in balance.

– Thirteen-year-old boy and electronic game lover

Think about karma in terms of your bank account with debits and credits. Transactions are the experiences that add to and take away from your third dimensional life on Earth. And the most critical element that comes into play is your perception and evaluation of these experiences.

One might look at my wheelchair and see a dead end. Not me, God. I say, "Thanks for the experience." I'm happy with the lessons my wheels have given me. I've taken my karma points earned from my disability and have created great things from it. This is my fourth book. I speak to thousands of people each year and it took a wheelchair to find the man I love! Steve and I met three years after my accident. We were in Jefferson City, the capital of Missouri, asking for funding to allow people with disabilities to stay in their own homes and not be warehoused in nursing homes. Nursing homes have their place but I was twenty-five when I was paralyzed and dreamed of my independence.

Because I have accepted what has transpired, I have abundance and joy in my life. Is everything in my life perfect? Far from it! But in the grand scheme it's all good!

When something appears to be going wrong, our first response is often, "Why me?" Then we become depressed, buying into fear, sadness, and misery, when instead, we should be asking, "Why not me?" We give away our power with thoughts of:

"This won't work."

"I can't do that."

"Why even try?"

These thoughts delete our karma account and they take away possibilities when the real questions should be: "What is the lesson here?" "What can I do to make the most of what is present?"

These thoughts lead us to find ways to not only survive, but thrive! Look for ways to add to the beauty of life. By appreciating what you have and thanking God and those around you for *it,* you bring more of ***it*** to you. Check out the 2000 movie *Pay it Forward*. It will help you realize that what you do makes a difference.

ADDING TO YOUR KARMA ACCOUNT

I am aware of karma through my everyday activities and my reactions to them. Whether conscious or unconscious, our thoughts and actions emit a vibration of energy through the Universe. Those energies attract like energies back to the source. Peaceful, happy, and loving energies vibrate at the highest frequencies while negative energies vibrate at low frequencies. Even the most dismal day has purpose.

– Chiropractor and mother

BREATHE When you have to make a decision or life throws you something unexpected, breathe. Take a deep breath; hold it, and then exhale. Slow yourself down for a minute to breathe and then make your necessary decisions.

LISTEN Trust your intuition and gut feelings. They often happen with a reason. I like to think of intuition as an internal judge. We know what's right and wrong for us and our interpretation affects our decisions.

BEAUTY Leave things better than you found them. Put forth an effort to make Earth a beautiful place to live for everyone and everything.

SPIRIT Aspire to be more spiritual. This is different from practicing a religion, which has a tendency to conquer and divide. Value everyone because everyone and everything has much to teach. The Creator will never dish out more than your soul can handle.

PACE Slow down the "monkey mind" on a treadmill, those hyper thoughts that fill your head and get in the way of clear thinking. Take time to be alone in thought through meditation or prayer. Be by yourself. Trust the God in you and slow down enough to listen.

FORGIVE	Let go of the past and forgive whoever did whatever. Let go of grudges and grow from the experiences.
ACCEPTANCE	What life sends you is the teacher. Be grateful for the lesson and move on.
DO IT	Eliminate "trying" and just do it or don't do it. Make a commitment either way.
SPOTLIGHT	Instead of focusing on what's wrong, ask, "What's right?"
QUESTION	Instead of asking, "Why me?" ask, "Why not me?"
GRATEFUL	Learn the error and thank the Universe for providing it.
CONFIDENCE	Don't buy into fear. You are worthy of good. A quote from the movie *Dune*: "Fear is a mind killer."
RESPONSE	Decide from the heart. Willingly give of yourself. Being a team player, helping, assisting, supporting, and caregiving are ways to rack up karmic points and add to your karma account.

KEEP AN OPEN MIND

ARRANGE YOUR LIFE'S HAPPINESS

REKINDLE LOVE OF SELF

MAKE YOUR OWN WAY

ALLOW TIME TO TEACH AND HEAL

DIFFERENT ABILITIES

Upon incarnation, you are given a mind, body, and spirit. We are here because of past karmic debt. Our soul has lessons to learn and we can develop mastership over physical existence through the power of spirit. This has helped me endure twenty years in my wheelchair. I have come to be grateful for every burden I've been given. Those burdens have been excellent teachers.

My nephew Dan is developmentally delayed and profoundly mentally disabled. He can't do a darn thing to knowingly help himself. But Dan is a wonderful example of compassion. He teaches us how to love unconditionally and how to give to those in need. Dan can say one word and it's a wonderful word. In a clear voice Dan will say, "Hi." He says it all the time—when he's with us out shopping, swimming at a pool—anywhere. People can't help but say, "Hi" in response.

It is my opinion that people with Down syndrome, a form of mental retardation, are often so loving that they do not create karma. They can be teachers of love and teach us to just "be." One time when I coordinated a weekend campout, two young boys with Down syndrome attended the outing. They just wanted to stay in their sleeping bags and hug each other all day so we did a little redirecting and all went well.

About a year after my auto accident, I started speaking at my niece's and nephew's schools about how I live with my disability. That is how my book *Aunt Katie's Visit* was born. The following year, I began living independently and hiring my own caregivers. Ten years later, I wrote *The Personal Care Attendant Guide*. I started sharing my poetry in my speeches and wrote *A Pocket of Poems and How to Write Your Own*. I would have never become an author if I had not become a woman on wheels, and again, it took a wheelchair to find the man I love. Woo hoo!

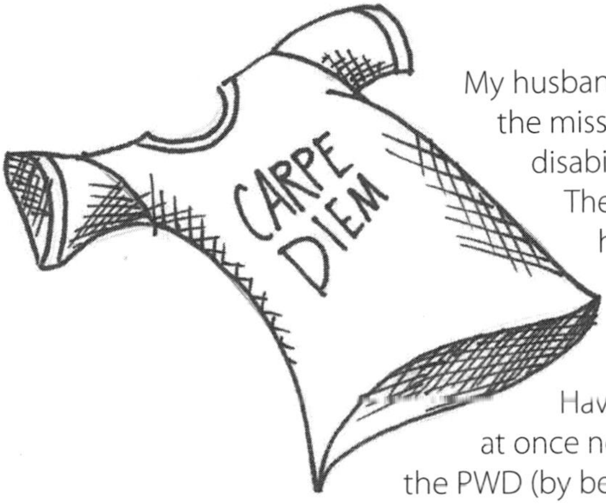

My husband Steve has this to say: "I think the mission of the souls of people with disabilities (PWD) is very interesting. The God-self of the PWD, chose to have this experience to challenge its own soul. PWD are burning off karma by taking on severe and/or multiple disabilities. Having such intense experiences all at once not only helps the soul growth of the PWD (by being a beacon to attract caregivers and family and offer opportunities to be good helpers), but also helps those around them have an opportunity to offer assistance, love, light, and human connection. Also, for the PWD, this is a test for free will: Do I accept this experience with a smile and deal with it or do I keep that "disability chip" firmly on my shoulder and say, 'Woe is me?', thus attracting more negativity and darkness my way?"

I think disabilities are opportunities to strengthen the character of one's soul. Likewise for those who support people with disabilities: family members, caregivers, teachers, etc. Doing the best you can under arduous circumstances is a testing ground for growth on a physical, cognitive, sensory, psychiatric and spiritual level.

Finally, from the Web site DailyOM.com: "Compassion is the ability to see the deep connectedness between ourselves and others. True compassion recognizes that all the boundaries we perceive between ourselves and others are an illusion. When we first begin to practice compassion, this very deep level of understanding may elude us, but we can have faith that if we start where we are, we will eventually feel our way toward it. We move closer to compassion every time we see past our own self-concern to accommodate concern for others. And, as with any skill, our compassion grows most in the presence of difficulty."

KARMA'S NOT FOR ME

The idea that there is some force in the Universe called karma that makes sure that everything is rewarded or punished in order to insure justice I feel is only wishful human thinking. If karma really existed there would be no need for police, courts, or social systems of any kind because karma would make sure everybody got what they deserved–good or bad–in the end.

– Philosopher and music lover

I am a Christian and do not believe in karma. I do believe that God created me with a "free will." I am responsible for the choices I make in life, whether good or bad. I also believe that sometimes bad things happen to good people. As a believer in the Bible, I believe in salvation, not reincarnation.

– Education coordinator and children's advocate

One of my friends had this to say:

"The popular TV show *My Name is Earl* is all about karma, but I don't believe in karma and here's why:

Who defines what good is?

If good is done to get good, does it then become a bad thing because it is for selfish gain?

Who defines when it crosses that line?

I know of wonderful people who have done untold good to and for others, but suffer from terrible diseases or hardships in their own life.

Everyone has some good and some bad in their life, so how do you know if it's from karma or not?

And is karma proportional? If you're a little bad, you only get a little bad in return?

What I do believe is that there are spiritual laws at work in the Universe and they are as real as gravity. I do believe in the "favor" of God (since I proclaim Jesus God as my Lord and Savior), but unless you claim that favor it goes unused in your life. Favor does not mean that life will go without problems in this world, but that God can and "will cause all things to work together for good to those that love the Lord." A good book about this is *Your Best Life Now* by Joel Osteen.

I also believe in seed time, harvest or sowing, and reaping as a spiritual law. I guess a good example of this is if a farmer sows corn, corn grows. He doesn't have to guess what will come out of the ground; it's going to be corn. So if people sow discord and evil I think their lives tend to follow that course. All I know is that God is bigger than our little minds can comprehend. Our lives are like looking through a peep hole in a door and thinking we have the whole picture. I think there are untold spiritual forces, both good and bad at work in this world, but we can't really explain how or why."

Everyone has a different understanding and awareness of karma. My mother taught me that it is important to respect other's opinions and beliefs. At times, we all must agree to disagree.

Let's look at karma in play here. Every belief system has karmic values, although they may not use the same terms.

THE FOLLOWING ARE FROM THE SACRED READING ARCHIVE OF CHERAG'S LIBRARY:

NATIVE AMERICAN

"All things are our relatives; what we do to everything, we do to ourselves. All is really One."

(Black Elk)

BUDDHIST

"Hurt not others in ways you find hurtful."

(Tripataka Udnana-varga 5.18)

CHRISTIANITY

"Therefore all things whatsoever you desire that men should do to you, do you even so unto them; for this is the Law and the Prophets."

(Matthew 7:12)

JUDAISM

"What is hateful to you, do not do to your fellow man.
That is the law; the rest is commentary."

(Talmud, Shabbat 31a)

ISLAM

"Not one of you is a believer unless he desires for his brother
that which he desires for himself."

(Qu'ran, Sunnah)

HINDU

"This is the sum of the Dharma: do naught do unto others
that which would cause pain if done to you."

(Mahabharata 5:1517)

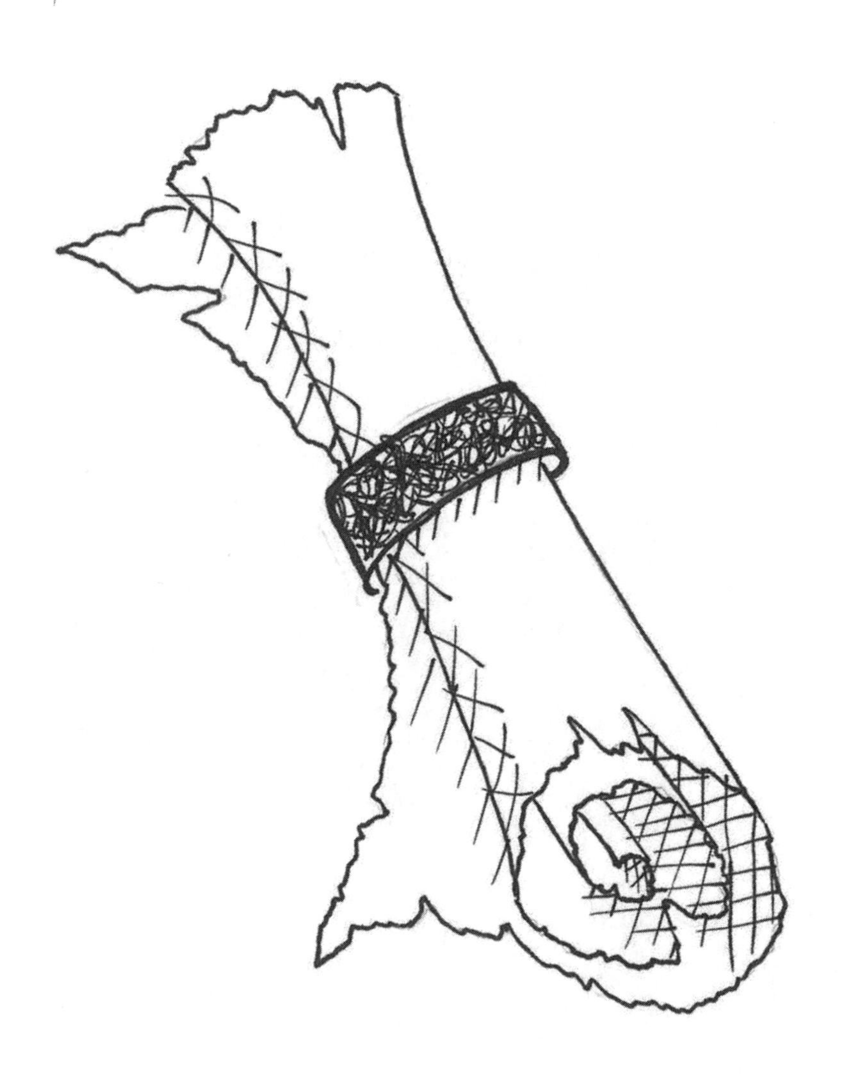

DEATH AND KARMA

I haven't finished this life just yet.
I'm sure the effects of karma will be much more visible
as I near the end of this particular journey.

– Business owner and actor

Losing a person or a pet hurts. It really hurts. God, does it hurt. But lose no faith; who we really are never dies. We simply take on a different form.

Our family celebrated a past Christmas at my house. It was a lovely holiday. The food was great, all eighteen of us could fit at a continuous table, and no one got mad at anyone else. Halfway through the evening I was in the kitchen and I experience a cold, cold, cold draft. In my best father's voice to my young nephews, I yelled, "You kids, shut the front door!" I turned around to see the door closed and not a kid in sight. I then felt the presence of my parents. It was too cool!

I've read in countless books that you can ask those who have passed on to visit you. I ask spirits who have passed on, "Will you visit me today and make your presence known in a way I will know it's you?" I meditate on the person and keep my mind open for any messages throughout the day. Maybe the radio plays their favorite song. Maybe you find a picture of them you didn't know you had. Maybe a cold blast of air goes through you and your next thought is about them.

I used to be afraid of dying. I just wasn't sure about it. But I've learned that who I am never dies! I am an eternal being. And I know I've been here before. I just know it. For example, about ten years ago I was viewing a replica of a slave ship at the St. Louis Science Center. I had the option of touring it from the owner's perspective or the slave's perspective. I chose the latter. I rolled through it slowly and came upon a drawing of how the slaves were positioned at the bottom of the huge ship, squeezed together, laying in their own filth. The tears rolled down my cheeks as I was paralyzed even more by this picture.

Steve comforted me and we finished experiencing the exhibit. About five months later I went to see a past life intuitive. She can see past lives. (Yes, I believe in that too.) She asked me a few questions and I told her that I felt I had been a slave in a former life. After moments of meditation, she informed me that I had died on board a slave ship during transit. I cried thinking again about the picture I had seen at the Science Center. It was pretty trippy!

One of my fears upon my own death is that I won't know what to do. But my fear has lessened after a very recent discussion with my friend Pat. She is a dear family friend who has Parkinson's disease. Years ago she brought me in to speak to her support group, The Movers and the Shakers. (I love that title.) Years later, we met up again at the fiftieth wedding anniversary celebration of mutual friends. Pat wobbled her way over and leaned on my wheelchair saying, "Katie, I had brain surgery last month and during the procedure I left my body. I saw former friends and family dressed in white. It was beautiful, just beautiful. Now, I am no longer afraid of dying." This sounds good to me because I've learned how to ask for help on this side; it's nice to know that it will be there on the other!

I've read in many sources that upon our death we go for our life's review. A great movie about this is called *Defending Your Life* with Albert Brooks and Meryl Streep. They go before a courtroom and re-experience every experience they had. Then, I guess you can decide to stay with your maker or return for another go-around. I would like to think that I'll chill out with God for a while but then again, I love mint chocolate chip ice cream, the warmth of the sun and the human experience.

Earth is our school and a place to become spiritually awakened. We must move beyond our wants and desires and seek spiritual development where there is no good or bad. There is what there is. Create from what is.

KARMIC FORGIVENESS

Karma is the responsibility of thoughts, deeds, and actions. Like a cannon being fired, it is the echo that goes on and on. Thoughts create things. Thoughts create karma. When others are mean we can choose to react by getting upset (which fuels the attacker) or we can send love and tell them we love them (or change the subject.) There is never a bad choice because you are responsible for your choices and everything is an experience.

– Free-loving soul and energetic healer

I know folks who love to play the blame game. These people are in their forties, fifties, and sixties and they are still mad at their parents for what they did or did not do when they were growing up. They have problems at work and blame it on their co-workers or supervisors. They blame their inabilities on society. Their problems are always someone else's fault and the reasons that they are unsuccessful in life, love, and the pursuit of happiness. It's like they are in a boat, sitting back, refusing to pick up a paddle and row. They are always mad about something and are champion grudge holders.

One of the best ways I have found peace in my life is to forgive. When something happens you must say to the Universe, "Thank you FOR GIVing me this experience." It's that simple because an attitude of gratitude leads to a loving and more accepting life – which is the essence of forgiveness. An attitude of gratitude is a beatitude. (Catholics live by seven principals as expounded in Matthew, Chapter 5 of the New Testament. Each principle begins with, "Blessed are the…" as a reminder to live a more loving life.)

When you hold a grudge, you give that person the power to control your reality. True forgiveness empowers you. You can do this. Because if I can, I

know you can. I could be a pretty mean and jealous person in my younger years and was often more angry than happy. My father was always angry about something too. But psycho-therapy helped me learn how to understand and better control my angry knee-jerk responses.

I have learned to forgive many people and situations. I've learned to bear the burden of some very tough decisions. I've learned to forgive with faith, and not fear; for hate destroys, while love builds. Now, there are days that suck, I mean they totally suck. But don't give up. Keep the faith, if not only for yourself but for those around you—your partner, your child, your pet, and everyone else. And forgive those who drive you crazy, for they have much to teach you.

Victor Wooten, a bass player, wrote my absolute favorite song of all time, "I Saw God" from the 2008 album *Palmystery*. In it he sings: "I saw God the other day. She look like you. He look like me."

I am God. You are God. We are all God! Isn't that cool? When we can see God in everything, we learn to be more forgiving beings. So go out there and love it ALL!

Existence is pure joy. We are so lucky to have the life we do and the ability to create the life we want. The opportunity is yours. Everything is an experience and provides the opportunity from which to learn and grow. Be present at all times because there is never "not now." We must let go of the past and live in the now. In the liner notes on the 1969 album ***Atlantis***, the jazz musician Sun Ra penned "The Dead Past":

"The civilizations of the past have been used as the foundation of the civilization today. Because of this, the world keeps looking toward the past for guidance. Too many people are following the past. In this new space age, this is dangerous. The past is DEAD and those who are following the past are doomed to die and be like the past. It is no accident that those who die are said to have passed since those who have PASSED are PAST."

Karma is getting your just due, based on actions for or against others.

– A recreation provider and lover of life

KARMA ACTION PLAN: NOW WHAT DO I DO?

There isn't good or bad, (but) our thinking makes it so.

—Joss Whedon, writer/producer/director of Firefly, Buffy the Vampire Slayer and The Doll House

If you believe that life is what you make of it, you are more than halfway there to building a better life for yourself. I've learned that an ounce of prevention is worth more than a pound of cure. Be proactive. Don't sit there waiting for life to happen to you. Instead, produce the life you want. Live, create, accept—and move on! How do I do this? I have four great coping mechanisms to share with you. Full participation, practiced on a regular basis, can help anyone succeed.

Feel It

I was never one to play poker. Why? Because I can't hide my feelings. When I'm happy, I laugh and when I'm sad, I cry. Unfortunately my father's response to my tears was always, "Quit crying or I'll give you something to cry about!" I hated hearing that and it made me cry even more, headfirst into my bed pillow. But it took me fifteen years of therapy to accept my salt water response to life's challenges and I continue to cry with pride. I even cry when I'm happy. I just feel better after a good cry. And I know crying isn't pretty; your eyes get red and swollen and you've got snot running from your nose. But that's the yucky stuff that needs to get out. So feel life and don't deny your feelings. Being able to feel is a wonderful gift to our souls while having our physical experiences. Don't deny your feelings, ever. They are lessons and opportunities to grow from. So, feel it!

Think It

Don't buy into fear. For some, fear can be more paralyzing than my spinal cord injury. Use therapy, hypnosis, or daily affirmations like, "I am healthy. I am safe." Release phobias and get out there. Prior to my paralysis, I spent most of my life feeling and then reacting. I never sat still. It was go, go, go, 24/7. I always worked two or three jobs at a time and I was a social butterfly with no limits. Consequently, I had shallow and empty relationships. I cheated on every guy I dated. I used them. They used me. I didn't slow down enough to think, until life slowed me down. My wheelchair causes me to think things through on a daily basis. I have to plan, organize, and process life on a daily basis. My body needs a lot of care and that requires an alert and patient mind. I don't recommend paralysis as a teacher of thought, but the Universe gave me what I needed. I hope you take time to think more, too. I know that thinking about a decision before I make it helps me make healthier, well-reasoned choices. So, think it!

Write It

All four of my books are a result of journal writing. Writing my thoughts, hopes, and aspirations allows me to empty my brain of chatter, fear, anxiety, and stress. It's like the trash truck that comes down our street. The truck grabs the can, electrically lifts it into the air, dumps the crap, and then releases the can. Ahh, the container is cleared out and ready for more. Dump your problems on a page. Don't edit, don't worry about spelling or punctuation. Just write extemporaneously. Vent, release, and think "thoughts leave my brain." I don't have a fancy journal, just a plain old notebook. But if you want to, buy a nice lined book and find a special pen or pencil to write with. Who knows what will come out of you! So, write it!

Say It

Seeing a counselor, psychiatrist, therapist or psychologist is one of the best gifts you can give yourself. Setting aside an hour a week, every two weeks, or once a month to meet with someone to improve your well-being is great mental health. I've met with grade school and college counselors, attended family group counseling, and continue to this day. I go to work on me. A good therapist listens and helps you find the answers. They put you in the driver's seat of your life. My therapist, Susan, was such a gift. She not only helped me to understand who I am, but also love who I am. I spent fifteen years with Susan when she and I agreed that I had fully accepted life. By that time, I had my husband Steve and was feeling quite strong. About a year later, I felt the need to go back into therapy and to find another therapist. It's OK to switch counselors if desire strikes or if you outgrow your therapist. But please, take care of your mental health. When you empty your brain by saying what's on your mind, your problems are not as insurmountable. I saw a quote on a bumper sticker that was attributed to Maggie Kuhn, a leader in the rights for the elderly. It read: "Speak your mind even if your voice shakes." You can get over what is ailing you. Just say it!

Your To-Do List

While you process life using my four-point coping strategy, I am also giving you a to-do list:

Pay attention to your surroundings	Do you like what you see?
Pay attention to those around you	Are you loving and sharing?
Pay attention to what goes into and out of your mouth	Are your words and foods healthy & loving choices?
Pay attention to time and how you use it	Do you share your time?
Pay attention to your intuition	Are you listening/following?
Pay attention to your thoughts	Are they helpful/healthy?
Pay attention to your decisions	Do you take time to reflect?
Pay attention to the present	Are you living in the NOW?

Because it is *never* not now!

Create the life you want and make the most of what you *do* have. I know life is tough. For ten years, I lived on food stamps and other public assistance. That situation was taxing and oftentimes very depressing. But I learned to be thankful for everything I had and everything I had been given. Throughout it all, and to this day, I choose to find the beauty in the bad and I know you can too.

Now go out into the Universe
and listen for your karmic validations.

– Rev. Katie Rodriguez Banister

Appendix A

THE 12 LAWS OF KARMA

(Adapted from Helion Publishing)

CAUSE AND EFFECT

As you sow, so shall you reap. The great Law of You Get What You Give.

You attract what you are, not what you want. Law of Creation. Your participation affects the outcome. Your surroundings are clues to inner nature.

What you resist persists for you. Law of Humility. What you object to reflects who you are inside. Are you lost in the illusion and deny who you are?

Wherever you go, there you are. Law of Growth. If you don't change, nothing is changed. Slowly learned changes, made in the heart, are the ones that last.

PERSONAL ACTION

Whenever there is something wrong, there is something wrong in you. Law of Mirrors. Are you contributing and making a difference in a loving way?

Whatever you do may seem insignificant, but it's important that you do it. Law of Synchronicity. Learn discipline and humility. We all count and we are one.

You can't think of two things at the same time. Law of Direction and Motives. Do you foster hidden agendas for personal gain or think beyond yourself?

If you believe something to be true, then sometime in life, you must demonstrate that truth. Law of Willingness. Afraid of hard work? Put up or shut up.

HISTORY AND RESULTS

You can't go home again. Law of Be Here Now. Let go of the past and move on.

The more things change, the more they stay the same. Law of Change. History repeats itself until you learn the lessons that change your path.

When you focus on your life, good things happen. Law of Patience and Reward. Do you focus on what you don't have? Do you seek the flashy instead of the basics? Joy comes from doing what you're supposed to do no matter how simple or grand.

What you put in, you get back. Law of Value and Upliftment. Whatever you contribute will uplift or decrease the whole. The value is the energy extended.

There are many universal laws that I have not included. If you want to pursue universal laws in depth, I suggest *Your Life: Why it Is the Way it Is and What You Can Do About It; Understanding The Universal Laws* by Bruce McArthur.

Appendix B

LAWS OF GOD

(from "Know Them by Their Fruits," by El Morya/Mark and Nada-Yolanda)

Oneness: God is one. As children of God we are one within ourselves and one with one another. In God and in I Am consciousness, separation cannot exist.

Equality: All are created equal and must be given equal opportunity to evolve and to express I Am consciousness.

Cause and effect: As we sow, so we will reap. As we give, so we will receive.

Compensation: Also called the Law of Give-and-Take. When we receive aid from another, sometime in our eternal ongoing we must give as we have received.

Noninterference: God has given each of us free will. Although we may educate or guide, we may not interfere with another's free will choices even when such are in error.

Divine will: We have free will and temporarily may disobey divine will. But eventually God's will must be done, regardless of how long it takes.

Example: Man learns through example. We demonstrate as examples for those of lesser consciousness, and learn from the examples of those who are ahead of us in spiritual growth.

Growth: Everything in creation is changing and evolving. We have unlimited opportunities for growth. But we alone can change ourselves.

Attraction: Like attracts like. What we concentrate on, we magnetically draw to ourselves.

Perfection: God is perfect. God creates and sees only perfection. Error can have no real or permanent existence.

Sacrifice: In order to fulfill our highest spiritual potential, we must sacrifice ourselves for the good of another.

Love: Love God and love one another.

BIBLIOGRAPHY

Chaney, Earlyne and Robert. Akashic Records. Upland, CA: *Astara*, 1996.

Dyer, Wayne W., PhD. *Ambition to Meaning*. Carlsbad, CA: Hay House, January 2009.

El Morya/Mark and Nada-Yolanda. "Know Them by Their Fruits." Pioneer, TN: Mark-Age, 1985.

"The Golden Rule." The Sacred Readings Archive.

http://www.Cheraglibrary.org/archive/md-004.htm.

Kuhn, Herman. *Karma - The Mechanism*. Incline Village, NV: Crosswind Publishing, 2001.

Kuhn, Maggie. "Speak Even if Your Voice Shakes." Bumper sticker. Minneapolis: Northern Sun, 2009.

Maslow, A.H. "A Theory of Human Motivation." *Psychological Review* 50(4) (1943):370-96.

Osteen, Joel. *Your Best Life Now – 7 Steps to Living Your Full Potential*. New York: Warner Faith First Trade Publishing, 2007.

Sun Ra. "The Dead Past." Back cover of *Atlantis*, compact disc. Conshohocken, PA: Evidence Music, 1993.

"Universal Laws." Chart. Tulsa, OK: Helion Publishing, 2000.

Wooten, Victor. "I Saw God the Other Day." *The Moses Code*, DVD. Carlsbad, CA: Hay House, 2008.

ONLINE RESOURCES

DrWayneDyer.com

Dr. Dyer's website, books, information and words of wisdom.

Astara.org

A site dedicated to elevating the spiritual consciousness and health of humankind.

CheragLibrary.org/archive/md-004.htm

A Sermon delivered by Rev. Hamid Cecil Touchon at the Church of All in Pagosa Springs, Colorado on January 8, 1995.

DeeperMind.com/20maslow.htm

Maslow's Hierarchy of Needs is an important psychological theory originated by American psychologist Abraham Maslow.

TheNewEarth.org/markage.html

Mark-Age, Inc. is a nonprofit spiritual-educational organization founded in 1960. Their teachings are based upon the interdimensional communications of Nada-Yolanda, a prophet for the New Age and the Second Coming.

MOVIE RECOMMENDATIONS

What The Bleep Do We Know?

Released in 2004, this documentary is a blend of science and religion that addresses quantum physics and our personal responsibilities to create the life we want.

The Secret

A fantastic film about the Law Of Attraction.

The Moses Code

Learn how to use the Law Of Attraction to do more than attract goods into your life, such as bringing goodness into the world.

I Heart Huckabees

A married couple help solve universal mysteries. Starring Dustin Hoffman and Lily Tomlin.

Harold and Maude

Harold is obsessed with death, Maude is obsessed with life. A love story and cult classic starring Bud Cort and Ruth Gordon.

Movies by Spiritual Cinema

Spiritual Cinema movies are uplifting stories that inspire love and compassion, films that connect us with the world around us.

ABOUT THE AUTHOR

In 1990, Katie Rodriguez Banister survived an auto accident that left her a quadriplegic, paralyzed from the chest down. After six months of rehabilitation and 15 months residing with her parents, she returned to living independently in 1992.

Katie worked as the Access Coordinator for the City of Webster Groves, Missouri, for five years. Prior to her accident, she was a latch-key director, a sales representative, a customer support representative, and social director.

Katie and her husband Steve co-founded Access-4-All, LLC, with a mission to educate and empower others through motivational speaking and disability education programs. Katie has authored *Aunt Katie's Visit* (2003), an educational book for children, which has been enjoyed equally by parents, teachers, and librarians.

Katie has also authored *The Personal Care Attendant Guide: The Art of Finding, Keeping or Being One* (2007). In 2008, Access-4-All published *A Pocket of Poems and How to Write Your Own*, a collection of stories, poems, and illustrations to encourage others to write as a coping mechanism.

A person who gives back to her community, Katie has been a member of the Recreation Council of the Greater St. Louis Board of Directors since 1992, where she has served two terms as president. She was also a board member of Lifeskills in St. Louis and a member of the Access Board with St. Louis Community College. Katie has been a board member of the Delta Center for Independent Living and has served as its president. In addition, she has been a board member of VSA Arts of Missouri. Katie was a performer and founding member of St. Louis' "DisAbility Project" and co-produced her own motivational video, "Change Takes Time." Katie has been featured in local newspapers numerous times for her dedication to educating the community.

KATIE'S HONORS INCLUDE

2010 Ms. Wheelchair Missouri

2001 St. Louis Woman of Achievement

Missouri Jaycees 1998 Ten Outstanding Young Missourians

St. Louis Jaycees Jr. Chamber of Commerce
1995 Ten Outstanding Young St. Louisans

Missouri Governor's Council on Disability 1993 Advocate of the Year

Central Missouri State University Outstanding Freshman
in the Department of Recreation 1983–84

Kirkwood, Missouri 1982 Junior Miss

In addition to her responsibilities as president of Access-4-All, LLC, Katie is a dynamic speaker, author, consultant, and disability educator. You can reach Katie at her Web site, www.access-4-all.com, or by e-mailing her at Katie@access-4-all.com.

MORE GOOD READING

FROM ACCESS 4 ALL, LLC

A Pocket of Poems – and how to Write your Own

An autobiographical collection with illustrations, stories and writing tips

Read Katie's stories and poetry about putting her life back together after a devastating accident and the lessons she learned along the way. Then, grab pen and paper and enjoy the ride as this Woman on Wheels teaches you how to express your own stories through poetry!

Aunt Katie's Visit

A modern look at disabilities for K-5

A valuable resource for parents and teachers to help children develop acceptance of others and good citizenship. This colorful, upbeat hardcover storybook is ideal for starting a conversation about differences and abilities. After Katie's visit, one second grader remarked, "LIfe isn't easy, but keep on going!"

Personal Care Attendant Guide

On the business of caregiving

Written by an inspiring speaker and advocate who is herself disabled, this guide teaches readers how to find a competent caregiver. It also gives current and prospective attendants vital information and real-life examples to help them succeed in this demanding work envoronment. Special features include: easy-to-use forms and worksheets, personal stories from people with disabilities who use attendants, anecdotes from experienced caregivers and resources listed alphabetically by disability. Published by Demos Medical Publishing.

Let Us Tailor A Program To Your Organization

Access-4-All's candid and informative presentations are an inspirational, motivational learning experience for all!

Katie Rodriguez Banister works well as your opening keynote and/or closing keynote speaker. She can deliver the opening motivational message to engage your conference attendees to get them excited. She can wrap up your conference with an inspirational closing speech to send your people on their way. Attendees will learn how to make change work, utilizing resources and interactive activities by identifying their strengths. We can also design educational programs for any grade level—students or faculty!

Staff Training, Retreats, Workshops, Business Conferences, Meetings, Keynotes

www.Access-4-All.com

ACCESS-4-ALL, INC. BOOK ORDER FORM

If this is a library book, please photocopy this form

Name/Company____

Address____

City_______________________________ State________ Zip______________

Day Phone___________________________ Fax_________________________

Email Address____

SHIP TO____

Address____

City_______________________________ State________ Zip______________

Mail Order Along with Payment To:

Access-4-All, llc P.O. Box 220751 St. Louis, MO 63122-0751

PRICING:

Shipping/Handling US Media Mail $5.00/+ $2 per additional book

Karmic Validations

Quantity __________ Retail $16.95 MO Tax (.06925) $ 1.17 = $18.12

Pocket of Poems

Quantity __________ Retail $19.95 MO Tax (.06925) $ 1.38 = $21.33

Aunt Katie's Visit

Quantity __________ Retail $16.99 MO Tax (.06925) $ 1.17 = $18.16

Personal Care Attendant Guide

Quantity __________ Retail $16.95 MO Tax (.06925) $ 1.17 = $18.12

Autographed/To Whom____

____

Payment: __ Cash __Check __Visa __MasterCard __Discover

Card Number ____

Expiration Date ________/_________ CVV number (3 on back) ______________

Name on the Card ____

Web Orders: www.Access-4-All.com